CAT'S REVENGE II

More Uses for Dead People

by Hodge

Illustrated by Jeff Danziger

Produced by Philip Lief

A **WALLABY** BOOK

Published by Simon & Schuster

NEW YORK

D1453707

OTHER BOOKS BY HODGE:
CAT'S REVENGE
HOW TO MAKE LOVE TO A CAT
MORE CAT TALES, STARRING HODGE

Published by Wallaby Books
A Simon & Schuster Division of
Gulf & Western Corporation
Simon & Schuster Building
1230 Avenue of the Americas
New York, New York 10020
WALLABY and colophon are registered
trademarks of Simon & Schuster
First Wallaby Books printing March 1982
Manufactured in the United States of America
10 9 8 7 6 5 4 3 2 1
ISBN 0-671-44805-6

I am not an especially vindictive creature. There are many things I would rather do than sit around and dream up uses for dead cat haters. After my first book, CAT'S REVENGE, came out, I was ready to withdraw my claws and let bygones be bygones — provided The Enemy was willing to do the same. But it soon became clear that the evil forces of ailurophobia were determined to wreak further havoc on innocent felines and their friends. So I had no choice but to step forward and once again defend the honor of my kind.

Fur standing on end, and fired with righteous anger, I returned to the drawing board to devise a second counter-attack. At first, I worked fast and furiously, but gradually I started to slow down. Why rush? With nine lives to The Enemy's one, time was on my side. As I worked, I began to feel much better, and by the time I was finished, I was purring contentedly.

There are many varieties of vengeance, but perhaps none so sweet as CAT'S REVENGE II.

Hodge

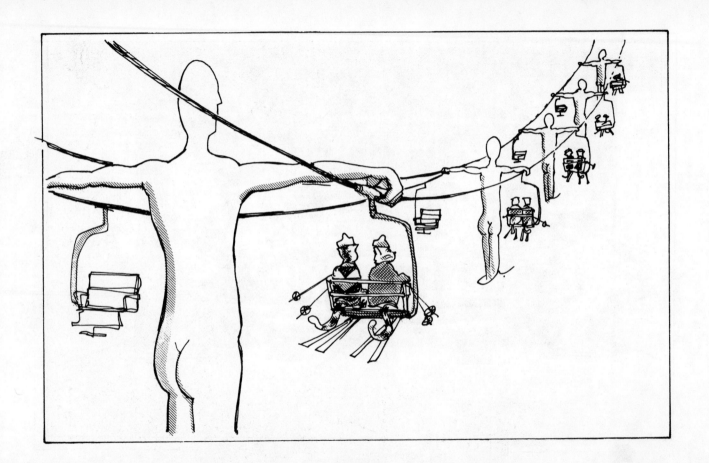

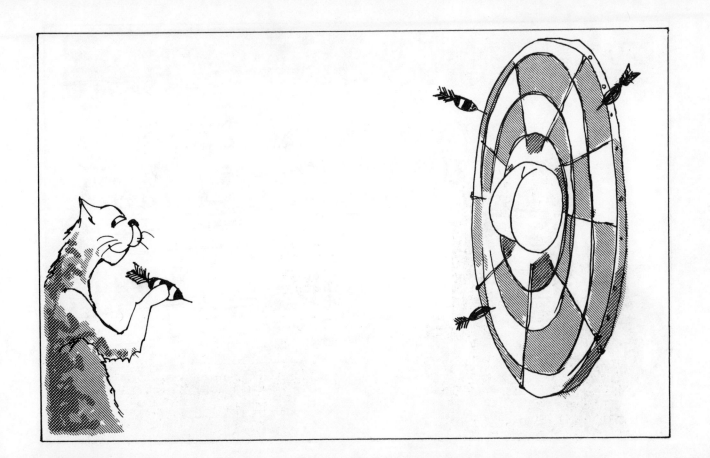

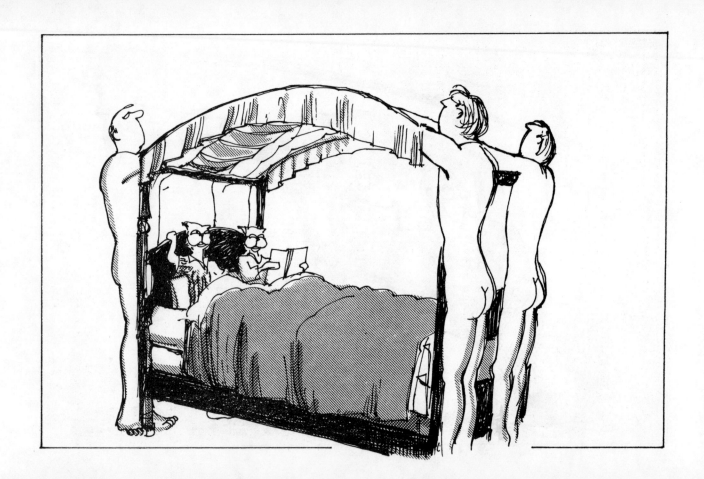

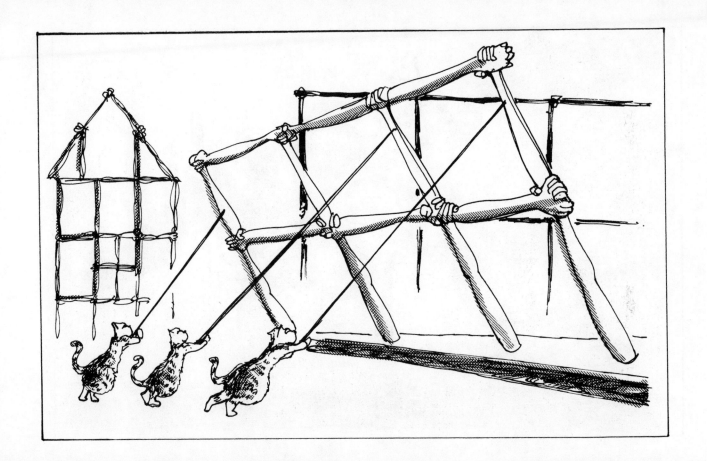

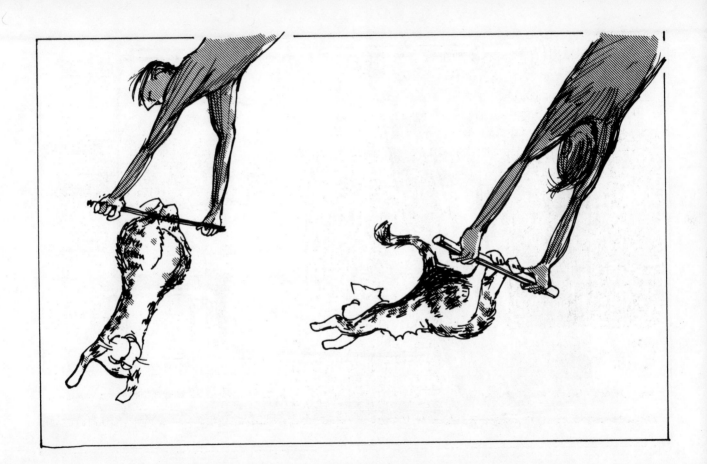

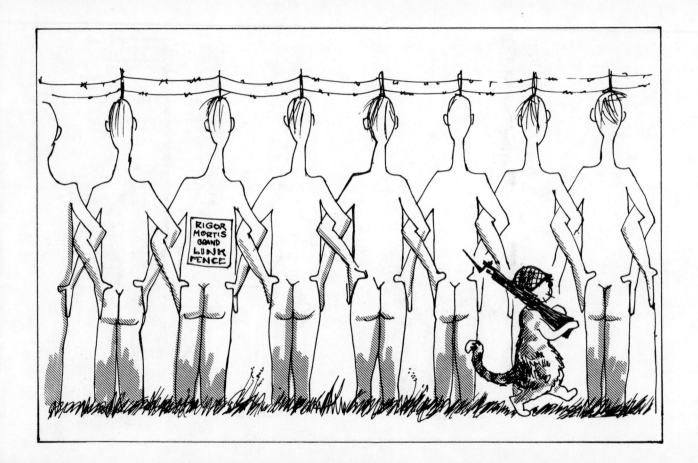

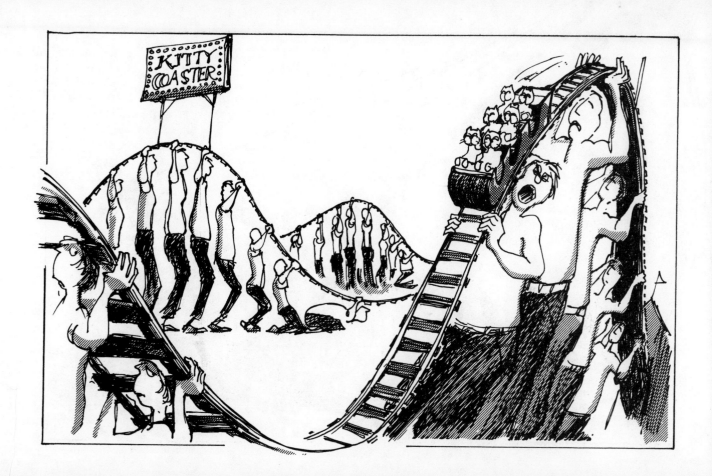

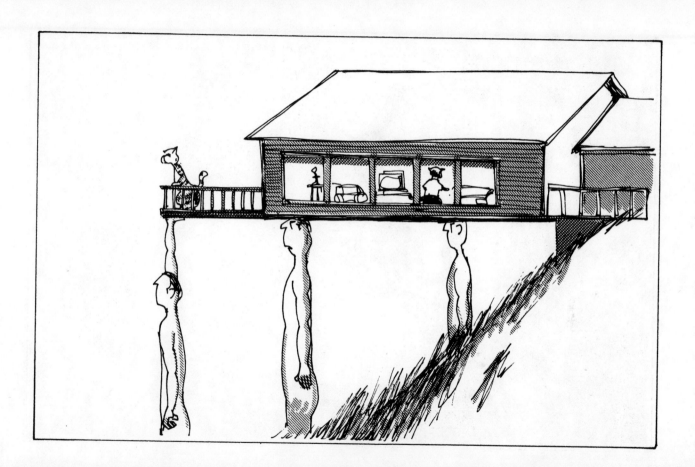